Paul Durcan was born in Dublin in 1944, of Co. Mayo parents. He studied archaeology and medieval history at University College Cork. In 1974 he won the Patrick Kavanagh Award and he received Creative Writing Bursaries from the Arts Council of Ireland in 1976 and 1980. He has given readings of his poems throughout the world. In 1981 he represented Ireland at the Struga Poetry Festival in Yugoslavia and in 1983 undertook a tour of the Soviet Union at the invitation of the Union of Soviet Writers. In May 1985 he was resident poet at The Frost Place, New Hampshire. He is a member of Aosdána.

Among Durcan's published works are:

Endsville (with Brian Lynch), New Writers Press, Dublin, 1967

O Westport in the Light of Asia Minor, Anna Livia Press, Dublin 1975

Teresa's Bar, Gallery Press, Dublin, 1976

Sam's Cross, Profile Press, Dublin, 1978

Jesus, Break His Fall, Raven Arts Press, Dublin, 1980

Ark of the North, Raven Arts Press, Dublin, 1982

The Selected Paul Durcan, Blackstaff Press, Belfast, 1982 (Poetry Ireland Choice), 1985

Jumping the Train Tracks with Angela, Raven Arts Press, Dublin/Carcanet New Press, Manchester, 1983

The Berlin Wall Café
Paul Durcan

THE
BLACKSTAFF
PRESS
BELFAST AND DOVER, NEW HAMPSHIRE

ACKNOWLEDGEMENTS

Adrift (New York); *Cyphers; Gown; Image;* the *Irish Press* (New Irish Writing); the *Irish Times; Magill; Paris/Atlantic*

I should like to acknowledge also the Tyrone Guthrie Centre at Annaghmakerrig and, in particular, to express my gratitude to Bernard and Mary Loughlin.

First published in 1985
by The Blackstaff Press Limited
3 Galway Park, Dundonald, Belfast BT16 0AN, Northern Ireland
and
51 Washington Street, Dover, New Hampshire 03820 USA
with the assistance of
The Arts Council of Northern Ireland

Printed in Northern Ireland
by The Universities Press Limited

British Library Cataloguing in Publication Data
Durcan, Paul
The Berlin Wall café.
I. Title
821'.914   PR6054.U72

Library of Congress Cataloging-in-Publication Data
Durcan, Paul, 1944–
The Berlin Wall Café.
I. Title.
PR6054.U72B4   1985   821'.914   85–19989

ISBN 0 85640 348 2

The world is a wedding

– The Talmud

CONTENTS

Part I

Part II

PART
I

The Haulier's Wife Meets Jesus on the Road Near Moone

I live in the town of Cahir,
In the Glen of Aherlow,
Not far from Peekaun
In the townland of Toureen,
At the foot of Galtee Mór
In the County of Tipperary.
I am thirty-three years old,
In the prime of my womanhood:
The mountain stream of my sex
In spate and darkly foaming;
The white hills of my breasts
Brimful and breathing;
The tall trees of my eyes
Screening blue skies;
Yet in each palm of my hand
A sheaf of fallen headstones.
When I stand in profile
Before my bedroom mirror
With my hands on my hips in my slip,
Proud of my body,
Unashamed of my pride,
I appear to myself a naked stranger,
A woman whom I do not know
Except fictionally in the looking-glass,
Quite dramatically beautiful.
Yet in my soul I yearn for affection,
My soul is empty for the want of affection.
I am married to a haulier,
A popular and a wealthy man,
An alcoholic and a county councillor,
Father by me of four sons,
By repute a sensitive man and he is
Except when he makes love to me:
He takes leave of his senses,

Handling me as if I were a sack of gravel
Or a carnival dummy,
A fruit machine or a dodgem.
He makes love to me about twice a year;
Thereafter he does not speak to me for weeks,
Sometimes not for months.
One night in Cruise's Hotel in Limerick
I whispered to him: Please *take* me.
(We had been married five years
And we had two children.)
Christ, do you know what he said?
Where? Where do you want me to take you?
And he rolled over and fell asleep,
Tanked up with seventeen pints of beer.
We live in a Georgian, Tudor, Classical Greek,
Moorish, Spanish Hacienda, Regency Period,
Ranch-House, Three-Storey Bungalow
On the edge of the edge of town:
'Poor Joe's Row' –
The townspeople call it –
But our real address is 'Ronald Reagan Hill',
– That vulturous-looking man in the States.
We're about twelve miles from Ballyporeen
Or, as the vulture flies, about eight miles.
After a month or two of silence
He says to me: Wife, I'm sorry;
I know that we should be separated,
Annulled or whatever,
But on account of the clients and the neighbours,
Not to mention the children, it is plain
As a pikestaff we are glued to one another
Until death do us part.
Why don't you treat yourself
To a week-end up in Dublin,
A night out at the theatre:
I'll pay for the whole shagging lot.

4

There was a play on at the time
In the Abbey Theatre in Dublin
Called *The Gigli Concert*,
And, because I liked the name –
But also because it starred
My favourite actor, Tom Hickey –
I telephoned the Abbey from Cahir.
They had but one vacant seat left!
I was so thrilled with myself,
And at the prospect of Tom Hickey
In a play called *The Gigli Concert*
(Such a euphonious name for a play),
That one wet day I drove over to Clonmel
And I went wild, and I bought a whole new outfit.
I am not one bit afraid to say
That I spent all of £200 on it
(Not, of course, that Tom Hickey would see me
But I'd be seeing myself seeing Tom Hickey
Which would be almost, if not quite,
The very next best thing):
A long, tight-fitting, black skirt
Of Chinese silk,
With matching black jacket
And lace-frilled pearl-white blouse;
Black fish-net stockings with sequins;
Black stiletto high-heeled shoes
Of pure ostrich leather.
I thought to myself – subconsciously, of course –
If I don't transpose to be somebody's *femme fatale*
It won't anyhow be for the want of trying.

Driving up to Dublin I began to daydream
And either at Horse & Jockey or Abbeyleix
I took a wrong turn and within a quarter-of-an-hour
I knew I was lost. I stopped the car
And I asked the first man I saw on the road
For directions:
'Follow me' – he said – 'my name is Jesus:

5

Have no fear of me – I am a travelling actor.
We'll have a drink together in the nearby inn.'
It turned out we were on the road near Moone.
(Have you ever been to the Cross at Moone?
Once my children and I had a picnic at Moone
When they were little and we were on one
Of our Flight into Egypt jaunts to Dublin.
They ran round the High Cross round and round
As if it were a maypole, which maybe it is:
Figure carvings of loaves and fishes, lions and dolphins.
I drank black coffee from a thermos flask
And the children drank red lemonade
And they were wearing blue duffle coats with red scarves
And their small round laughing freckled faces
Looked exactly like the faces of the twelve apostles
Gazing out at us from the plinth of the Cross
Across a thousand years.
Only, of course, their father was not with us:
He was busy – busy being our family euphemism.
Every family in Ireland has its own family euphemism
Like a heraldic device or a coat of arms.)
Jesus turned out to be a lovely man,
All that a woman could ever possibly dream of:
Gentle, wild, soft-spoken, courteous, sad;
Angular, awkward, candid, methodical;
Humorous, passionate, angry, kind;
Entirely sensitive to a woman's world.
Discreetly I invited Jesus to spend the night with me –
Stay with me, the day is almost over and it is getting dark –
But he waved me aside with one wave of his hand,
Not contemptuously, but compassionately.
'Our night will come' he smiled,
And he resumed chatting about my children,
All curiosity for their welfare and well-being.
It was like a fire burning in me when he talked to me.
There was only one matter I felt guilty about
And that was my empty vacant seat in the Abbey.
At closing-time he kissed me on both cheeks

And we bade one another Goodbye and then –
Just as I had all but given up hope –
He kissed me full on the mouth,
My mouth wet with aziliran lipstick
(A tube of Guerlaine 4 which I've had for twelve years).
As I drove on into Dublin to the Shelbourne Hotel
I kept hearing his Midlands voice
Saying to me over and over, across the Garden of
    Gethsemane –
Our night will come.

Back in the town of Cahir,
In the Glen of Aherlow,
Not far from Peekaun
In the townland of Toureen,
At the foot of Galtee Mór
In the County of Tipperary,
For the sake of something to say
In front of our four sons
My husband said to me:
Well, what was Benjamino Gigli like?
Oh, 'twas a phenomenal concert!
And what was Tom Hickey like?
Miraculous – I whispered – miraculous.
Our night will come – he had smiled – our night will come.

The Most Beautiful Woman in France

It is not every terminal cancer patient
Has a beautiful girlfriend
But Mann, who had about nine months to live,
Had a girlfriend who by general repute
Was the most intelligent woman in Paris
And the most beautiful woman in France.
There was no doubt that she knew
Mann was a terminal patient
But no one could work out if this was why
He occupied such a special place in her heart,
Or was it a rare occurrence of true love –
A genuine case of *amour*?
But then one day she solved the problem
For all us nosy-parkers
Lurking about the drawing-rooms of Paris
With our watering-cans poised over our potted spouses
When she dropped Mann like a crate
– A crate of bananas from Sierra Leone –
And advised him that she was not hooked on him anymore:
That's how she put it to him – noiselessly –
'Mann, I am not hooked on you anymore'.
Mann, it seems, had thought he had it all sewn up;
Mann had been resting on his laurels,
Basking under the yew tree;
Mann had rather complacently assumed
That his terminal cancer was a foolproof guarantee
That she'd stick by him, a sure-fire entrée
Into her boudoir on the Boulevard Haussmann.
Even if a man is facing certain death
He should keep on his toes.
There is at least one thing worse than certain death
And that's when immortal woman signals to mortal man
That she is not hooked on him anymore;
The orchids that would have arrived after your death

Start piling up at your door before your death:
Staring into the white, black-petalled void, hearing her
    whisper –
'Mann, I am not hooked on you anymore'.

Le Poète Allongé

(after Chagall)

I was lying flat on my back on the underground train
Going from one end of the Moscow Metro to the other
When a green-faced foreigner gets on at Pushkinskaya
And, wrapping his icy hands around my boney head,
He whispers 'Is there anything I can do for you?'
Holy Lenin! I felt like liquidating him on the spot.
Luckily there was a KGB lassie sitting beside him
And she told him briskly to mind his own business;
These foreigners never know when to leave well alone.
Besides, I was feeling pretty poleaxed at the time;
I would have needed several militiamen to get me to my
     feet.
I went back to sleep and through my half-open eyes
Dreamed of appropriating his foreign shoes.
Dexterously, while he scrutinized the Moscow Metro
– The Sinister Moscow Metro –
I untied his shoelaces and removed his shoes.
I knew also that as soon as he surfaced into Red Square
The militia would compliment him walking about in his red
     socks.
Red Square is the Most Beautiful Square in the   orld –
Krasnaya Ploshchad –
Where adult men and women, no matter how corrupted by
     the age,
Must all wear Little Red Shoes.
Red *is* Beautiful:
If the world had a heart, which it has,
The world would get married in Red Square,
Just like I myself got married in Red Square
When I was a young man in the Winter of 1952.
On our wedding-day we went to the Kremlin Wall
To lay a bouquet of mimosa beside the eternal flame
At the Tomb of the Unknown Soldier:

10

'Your name is unknown, your feet are immortal' –
Then in a fleet of three taxis we drove up into the Lenin Hills
And, looking back down northwards over Moscow,
Dark lovely Moscow,
We uncorked bottles of Georgian champagne in the sunny
    snow.
She divorced me three years later because she could not
    bear,
Quite rightly, my vodka-drinking.
I am drinking myself to death, but O Marina
What memories what smells drift back through the taiga!
Your small round laughing Siberian eyes
Are forever waiting for me at the end of the line
Where of course there is never a soul except me,
My proud silent horse, and my pig that never squeals.
When I get to the end of the line
I will give you a pair of new shoes;
I will leave in my will for your new man
A pair of American shoes.
Strange, Marina, isn't it, but as I recline here
On my back in the Metro
I think that the next world will be like America:
The next world will be like America, but this world is like
    Russia!

High-Speed Car-Wash

We were making love in the high-speed car-wash
When a most peculiar thing occurred:
I chanced to glance around momentarily
As we were readjusting our seat belts,
And what did I see but two nuns
Peering in the back window of my new Peugeot!
Obviously they were not aware that I could see them
And their faces were suffused in a kind of golden red
Sanctuary light as they stared in at us entranced:
The plush, emerald, furry rollers of the car-wash
Plied and wheeled and shuddered, backwards and
    forwards,
Crawling all over the body of the car.
We let ourselves be clawed in it, and by it,
Surrendering ourselves to it entirely,
Immersed, and yet not immersed, in its floods and suds,
Flowing into one another like Christ flowing into the Cross,
In one another's throats soaking together.
As we drove off, the car was dripping wet,
And the two nuns in black were gleaming in the sun,
Each with, in her hands behind her back,
A rolled-up red umbrella twirling to and fro,
Snatches of converse floating on the air:
– It's a lovely-looking car, really, isn't it, the new Peugeot?
– Oh it is. . . I thought it looked lovely in the car-wash.
And I said to Maeve Smith: Maria Callas, –
    didn't she really have a truly divine voice?
And Maeve Smith said to me: Yes, but do you know
    that her real name was Maria Anna Kalageropoulos?

Bewley's Oriental Café, Westmoreland Street

When she asked me to keep an eye on her things
I told her I'd be glad to keep an eye on her things.
While she breakdanced off to the ladies' loo
I concentrated on keeping an eye on her things.
What are you doing? – a Security Guard growled,
His moustache gnawing at the beak of his peaked cap.
When I told him that a young woman whom I did not know
Had asked me to keep an eye on her things, he barked:
Instead of keeping an eye on the things
Of a young woman whom you do not know,
Keep an eye on your own things.
I put my two hands on his hips and squeezed him:
Look – for me the equivalent of the Easter Rising
Is to be accosted by a woman whom I do not know
And asked by her to keep an eye on her things;
On her medieval backpack and on her spaceage Walkman;
Calm down and cast aside your peaked cap
And take down your trousers and take off your shoes
And I will keep an eye on your things also.
Do we not cherish all the children of the nation equally?
That woman does not know the joy she has given me
By asking me if I would keep an eye on her things;
I feel as if I am on a Dart to Bray,
Keeping an eye on her things;
More radical than being on the pig's back,
Keeping an eye on nothing.
The Security Guard made a heap on the floor
Of his pants and shoes,
Sailing his peaked cap across the café like a frisbee.
His moustache sipped at a glass of milk.
It is as chivalrous as it is transcendental
To be sitting in Bewley's Oriental Café
With a naked Security Guard,
Keeping an eye on his things

And on old ladies
With thousands of loaves of brown bread under their
    palaeolithic oxters.

The Man with Five Penises

My father was a man with five penises.
I caught a glimpse of him in the bath one morning,
A Sunday morning after Mass and Holy Communion
(Normally he went to Golf after Mass and Holy
    Communion
But owing probably to weather conditions
– Sand-bunkers flooded and greens waterlogged –
There was no Golf on the Sunday morning in question).
I stepped into the bathroom, thinking it empty:
There he was, immobile as a crocodile,
In communion with waters that looked immensely fishy.
He peered at me out of his amphibious eyes;
I stepped back out, as out of a jungle comic.
'I am having a bath' he growled fretfully.
I could have sworn I saw, as I say,
At least four or five penises floating about,
Possibly six or seven.
For a long time after that, I used feel sorry for him,
Concerned as well as sorry:
He must have a right old job on his hands every morning
Stuffing that lot into his pants.
And imagine what he must feel
When he has to use the public toilets,
Holding himself together for fear
All that lot might spill out –
What would the blokes in the next stalls say to him?
But also I began to worry about myself:
Maybe it was me who was all missing,
Me with my solitary member.
Over the next years I watched anxiously
For signs of new members
But membership remained steadfastly at zero.
Now that I know the score
– Or at least now that I think I know the score –
I am inclined to think

15

One penis is more than enough.
Although I will always cherish the notion
Of my father as the man with five penises,
Initially I interpreted it as a sinister spectacle
And frankly it comes as a relief to discover
That there was in fact only one of them.
Unquestionably, one penis is more than enough.

I Was a Twelve Year Old Homosexual

My lover was a freckled, curly-haired boy from Connemara,
Now a leading brain-surgeon in France
(I hear he has been married for almost twenty years
To an extremely nice man from Fontainebleau).
When the pair of us were twelve years of age
We used exchange love-notes in Religious Knowledge class
Until my Mother, poking in the pockets of my jackets,
Excavated a hoard of these transcendentally erotic bits of
      paper.
My Mother mocked me, and my Father flogged me.
The Head Priest took me for a long walk in the school
      woods,
In which, between black pregnant pauses, he whispered
      hoarsely:
It will have to stop!
I agreed and I gave up homosexuality,
Yet to this day I cannot recall without being just a little
      bashful
That in Ireland in the 1950s
I was a twelve year old homosexual!

The Man who Thought he was Miss Havisham

When a wife discovers that her husband is a transvestite
Normally after the initial shock she recovers
And, if she loves him, life returns to normal abnormal.
Often as not, it turns out that she is a transvestite also
And what was a jolly household becomes an ecstatic
 household
As the pace of the clothes-swapping hots up:
She slouching about in his battledress, quick on the draw;
He clicking about in her frocks, never slow to swoon.

Mind you, the odd row cannot be avoided:
He can get uppitty if she leaves him
Without a clean pair of Y-fronts;
She gets prickly if she finds
There is not a clean bra in the house.
At Sunday Mass, however, the pair of them
Are a model of decorum:
He in ankle-length evening gown
With yellow wig down to the waist;
She in fisherman's waders and oilskins,
Short back and sides.

But when I discovered that my husband
Thought of himself as Miss Havisham,
Well, old son, I could not wear it at all!
I blew a gasket, tripped the trip-switch!
I simply could not bear to watch him
Moping there in front of the ape-faced TV
In his wedding-dress,
Forever readjusting his trousseau,
Forever caressing the confetti on his shoulders,
Forever casting glances at the rose in his bosom.
For four years he lay there in front of the TV
Until I said to him through nailed teeth:
Miss Havisham, I will have you know

18

That you will have to leave this house.
Without a whimper he phoned for a Wedding Car –
The most expensive Wedding Hearse in Limerick City –
And committed himself into the local mental hospital
– Joyce Towers – where they keep him amused
With regular courses in Electric Convulsive Treatment
And month-long sessions of Nevada Group Therapy
(An up-market technique in brainwashing).
Once a year we get a postcard from him saying:
Having a lovely honeymoon – no shortage
Of spacemen – love and tears, Miss H.

Man Smoking a Cigarette in the Barcelona Metro

I was standing in the Metro in the Plaza de Cataluña
Waiting for the rush-hour train to take me home to Tibidabo
When, gazing and staring – as one does gaze and stare –
At the passengers on the opposite platform,
I saw a naked man smoking a cigarette.
I cannot tell you how shocked I was.
He was by no means the only passenger smoking a cigarette
But he was the only naked passenger smoking a cigarette.
It was like seeing a horse in the rush hour smoking in the
    crowd.
Although I was in a hurry to get home to Tibidabo
I was so shocked that I ran back down the stairs,
Past the buskers and the jasmine-sellers and the *Guardia
    Civil*,
And crossed the tunnel to the other side of the tracks.
I went straight up to him and with no beating about the
    bush
I expressed to him my indignation and my ideological
    position:
'I happen to regard the naked human body as sacred –
If you want to profane it by smoking a cigarette
Have the decency to put on some clothes
And go about your smoking like everyone else
In shame and concealment, in jeans and ponchos.
What do you think clothes are for but to provide an alibi
For perversity, a cover-up for unnatural practices?'
He snatched the cigarette from his mouth and threw it
    down into the tracks,
And immediately he looked like a human being
    metamorphosed –
He began to shake with laughter, whinnying, neighing –
As if he were the first horse on earth,
Sauntering up and down the platform of the Metro
All knees and neck,
The bells of his genitals tolling in the groin of time.

As he rode up and down the platform
In ones and twos and threes the women passengers
Began to fling their smoking cigarettes down into the tracks
And, as they did,
Their garments fell away from them
And they stepped out into themselves cigaretteless,
As with a new-born sense of pride and attraction.
In the end only all the men were left –
Fuming aliens –
Chain-smoking in their clobber,
Glaring with clumsy envy
At the naked man, cigaretteless,
Circled round by all of his newly-equipped fans
Fanning him with nothing but the fans of their bodies
Riding high on thigh-bone and wrist:
No longer hooked on trains, or appearances, or loss.

Bob Dylan Concert at Slane, 1984

'I saw close up the make-up on Bob Dylan's face!'
She confides into the dressing-table looking-glass in our
    bedroom,
Randy to report the felicity of what's morbid:
Mock-shock, sex-scandal, night-delight.

I glimpse the drenched pair of hips –
The drenched denimed pair of hips
Of the boy who, swimming across the river to get in,
Drowned. And while Bob Dylan and his Band –
And a hundred thousand fans –
Made noise that out-Táined the Táin,
The St John of Malta Ambulance Women
Fished out a corpse –
Cradled it in a stretcher and wrapped it round
In grey swaddling – prison issue.

They offloaded him into the White Ambulance,
As into a Black Maria, then off and away – with him –
To begin a life-sentence
For which there is no parole – no parole at all.
Not for nothing do men wear make-up
And poets ear-rings: not for nothing
Was Bob Dylan's noise noise, his music music.

The National Gallery Restaurant

One of the snags about the National Gallery Restaurant
Is that in order to gain access to it
One has to pass through the National Gallery.
I don't mind saying that at half-past twelve in the day,
In my handmade pigskin brogues and my pinstripe double-
    vent,
I don't feel like being looked at by persons in pictures
Or, worse, having to wax eloquent to a client's wife
About why it is that St Joseph is a black man
In Poussin's picture of *The Holy Family*:
The historical fact is that St Joseph was a white man.
I'd prefer to converse about her BMW – or my BMW –
Or the pros and cons of open-plan in office-block
    architecture.
I clench the handle of my briefcase
Wishing to Jesus Christ that I could strangle Homan
    Potterton –
The new young dynamic whizz-kid Director.
Oh but he's a flash in the pan –
Otherwise he'd have the savvy to close the National Gallery
When the National Gallery Restaurant is open.
Who does Homan Potterton think he is – Homan Potterton?

The Cabinet Table

Alice Gunn is a cleaner woman
Down at Government Buildings,
And after seven o'clock Mass last night
(Isn't it a treat to be able to go to Sunday Mass
On a Saturday! To sit down to Saturday Night TV
Knowing you've fulfilled your Sunday obligation!)
She came back over to The Flats for a cup of tea
(I offered her sherry but she declined –
Oh I never touch sherry on a Saturday night –
Whatever she meant by that, I don't know).
She had us all in stitches, telling us
How one afternoon after a Cabinet Meeting
(One of those afternoons when it gets dark so early
That the streetlamps are all lit up by 3.30 pm)
She got one of the Security Men
To lie down on the Cabinet Table,
And what she didn't do to him –
And what she did do to him –
She didn't half tell us;
But she told us enough to be going on with.
Do you know what it is? – she says to me:
No – says I – what is it?
It's Mahogany – she says – Pure Mahogany.

The Day Kerry Became Dublin

I was reading gas meters in Rialto
– In and out the keeled-over, weeping dustbins –
When, through the open doorway of the woman in the
    green tracksuit
Who's six feet tall and who has nine kids,
I heard a newsreader on the radio announcing
That the Bishop of Kerry had been appointed Archbishop of
    Dublin.
I couldn't help thinking that her bottom
Seemed to be independent of the rest of her body,
And how nice it would be to shake a leg with her
In a ballroom on a Sunday afternoon
Or to waltz with her soul at the bottom of the sea.
'Isn't that gas?' – she sizzles –
'Making the Bishop of Kerry the Archbishop of Dublin!'
Under her gas meter I get down on my knees
And say a prayer to the side-altars of her thighs,
And the three-light window of her breasts.
Excuse me, may I beam my torch in your crypt?
I go to Mass every morning, but I know no more
About the Archbishop of Dublin than I do about the Pope of
    Rome.
Still, I often think it would be
Uplifting to meet the Dalai Lama,
And to go to bed for ever with the woman of my dreams,
And scatter the world with my children.

Archbishop of Dublin to Film *Romeo and Juliet*

At the Jesus Palace in Drumcondra last night
At a heavily publicised, heavily laid-back, downbeat press
    conference
It was officially leaked to the Irish People
That the Archbishop of Dublin,
As evidence of his passion
To stamp out sexuality and spread the gospel of love
(Like butter across. . . the Golden Vale),
Is to direct a new film of *Romeo and Juliet*
In which not only at no point in the love story
Will the two bodies of Romeo and Juliet so much as touch –
Ouch! –
But at no point will they be in the same boat together
Or – 'to express ourselves cinematically', as the Jesus
    spokesman said –
In the same take together.
The Archbishop of Dublin,
Inspired by the example of Saint Samuel Beckett
– We were told –
Will isolate Romeo and Juliet
In separate refrigerators:
Romeo in a refrigerator in Rome,
And Juliet in a refrigerator in Armagh;
From which they will commune
By telephone. At the climax – of the film –
Intercourse will take place by television link,
Courtesy of Eurovision.
The reaction amongst international film critics
Is that not since *Last Tango in Paris*
(Last seen in Dublin in 800 AD)
Will the cinema have seen
As erotic a conception of sexual love
As the Archbishop of Dublin's *Romeo and Juliet.*
The film will be shot in the Jesus Palace
And on location in the Arctic Circle and Lough Derg.

Subtitled 'The Age of Ice'
Romeo and Juliet by the Archbishop of Dublin
Will go on general release next year
After a private showing. A tight lid is being kept
On news of the whereabouts of the private showing
Or as to the kind of private showing it is likely to be:
'A reasonably normal kind of private showing' –
Was all that the Jesus spokesman would say.
This is Marlon Brando in Dublin handing you back to the studio in
   Tahiti.

Archbishop of Kerry to Have Abortion

At a clandestine press conference in the Kerry Mountains,
Organised by the dissident playwright Dr Joe Pat Sheehy,
It was revealed that the Archbishop of Kerry,
Fifty-five year old Boethius Sheehy
(No relation to Dr Joe Pat Sheehy),
Having been made pregnant by a devoutly pious,
Over-sensitive member of the Nuns of the Big Flower,
Is to undergo an abortion next week
At the Vatican Abortion Clinic in Rome
Located in the apartments – whose blinds are always
    drawn –
Of the Congregation of the Propagation of the Defence of
    the Faith
Whose Acting Head at the present time is Cardinal Ian
    Paisley.
Archbishop Boethius –
Known affectionately to his flock as 'Yellowface' –
Is reported to be scared stiff of the forthcoming
    referendum –
I'm sorry, I'll read that again –
Is reported to be scared stiff of the forthcoming abortion.
But, despite appeals from nuns all over Kerry
(A Ballyferriter Sister is reputed to be the father),
The Vatican is adamant that the abortion must go ahead.
This is P.J. Newman in the Macgillacuddy Reeks
Handing you back – stociously, I mean stoically – to the studio in
    Dublin.

Acapulco

While the bishop was being installed on one side of the field
His daughter was being crucified on the other side of the
    field.
It was a lovely day, a sunny day in midwinter,
And everyone said how Christmassy it was –
In a messy, family kind of way.
Of course, the bishop didn't let on that he was her father
But she, formerly an adept in pastoral voodoo,
Began to perspire and gasp and bleed on the cross
And, as the bishop drove off in his bishopmobile,
She let the cat out of the bag by crying 'Father, Father'.

But he drove on, taking no notice of his crucified daughter,
Merely dreamily remarking to his new girlfriend
'Have you ever been to Acapulco?
I'm very pro-Acapulco'.

Three hundred years passed by before the bishop spoke
    again.
On a juicy, turquoise, laundered Summer's evening,
Perambulating alone in his private aerodrome,
In dignified, polite, adenoidal tones he uttered –
Audibly, so that the tubular-steel trees might hear him –
'I commanded my daughter to climb a tree but she
    disobeyed me,
So I crucified her and became a bishop and went to live in
    Acapulco:
Acapulco is what life's all about.'

The Feast of St Bridget,
Friday the First of February 1985

Don't suppose Derrylin will ever be prestigious as
    Auschwitz:
So what?

Funny to think that we're here living in Derrylin:
So what?

Doubt if anybody has ever heard of Derrylin:
Maybe so.

In Enniskillen and Armagh they'd know about Derrylin:
Maybe so.

But in Belfast or Dublin they'd not know about Derrylin:
Maybe so.

Conceivable that somebody in Mexico might know about
    Derrylin:
Maybe so.

A thirty-nine year old father-of-two in Derrylin:
So what?

What's a thirty-nine year old father-of-two?
In all my years in Mexico I never heard of such a thing.

Waiting to drive busload of Derrylin schoolkids to
    swimming pool:
So what?

Shot at the wheel, staggered up aisle of the bus, shot dead:
So what?

Killers cheered as they climbed out of bus into getaway car:
Maybe so.

Drove off across the Border into the Republic of Ireland:
Maybe so.

Children had to wait for three hours before removal of
    corpse:
So what?

Children had to step over pool of blood and broken glass:
So what?

But you know what children are like:
So what?

On the First Day of Spring, on the Feast Day of Saint
    Bridget.
Maybe so.

Catholic Father Prays for his Daughter's Abortion

Should that bank manager down in Connemara
Make my daughter pregnant and ditch her,
And should she dread
The prospect of being an unmarried mother,
I pray that she may find a nursing home
Tended with compassion by nursing nuns
In which she will be given the abortion that is her due.
When my other daughter told her boyfriend she was
    pregnant
He was scared stiff, but not that she was pregnant –
He felt chuffed at being verified a virile, feckless fellow –
What he was scared of was that he might have to do
Something about the consequences of being a virile,
    feckless fellow.
Society has a duty to the individual
As has the individual to society;
Long before my daughters graced this earth
Society, such as it is, had come into being,
Organised itself into the shambles that it is,
Where women are hard put to get away with life
But men get away with murder day by day.
I stare into the church candles flickering
Consolatorily in the dark, while outside
The snow piles up on the icy, gritted street.
I pray for my daughter's abortion and well-being
In the caring hands of a merciful God.
As I take my leave the parish priest with the heart of gold
Throws me a stealthily murderous scowl –
He knows that I pray to God and not to him –
And across the street an old woman is selling newspapers
    from a pram
And the snow is driving on – not leaping to greet me.

Bird-Watcher on Pigeon House Road

He is sitting at the wheel of a cream-white Porsche
Behind brown-tinted windows,
With a big black pair of field glasses raised to his eyes
In the twilight of a Spring evening,
Watching a container ship
Sailing upriver from the open sea
Before heaving itself around, broadsides,
To berth in the Alexandra Basin.
Nearby, in the coal dust and gull shit,
In and around the back wheels of the Porsche,
In the lee of their caravan,
Tinker children play 'donkey' –
Employing as a ball an empty tin of baked beans.
Across the harbour road outside her terrace house
An old woman says: 'Wha's tha' fella'?'
A neighbour woman whispers, confidentially:
'Him? Politics – Knights of Saint Patrick –
Big on the law and order – the birch, no less,
For tinkers and vandals – fair play to him.
They say he's dead keen on the bird-watching.'
The container ship berthed, he drives off
Across the city to his detached suburban residence
Where his wife and children are waiting to adore him.
As he sinks into his armchair by the fireside telly,
And his daughters help him to slip into his slippers
And his wife services him with steak and Brussels sprouts,
He feels a deep-seated sense of satisfaction
At the timely delivery of yet another ton of heroin.

10.30 am Mass, June 16, 1985

When the priest made his entrance on the altar on the stroke
   of 10.30
He looked like a film star at an international airport
After having flown in from the other side of the world,
As if the other side of the world was the other side of the
   street;
Only, instead of an overnight bag slung over his shoulder,
He was carrying the chalice in its triangular green veil –
The way a dapper comedian cloaks a dove in a silk
   handkerchief.
Having kissed the altar, he strode over to the microphone:
I'd like to say how glad I am to be here with you this
   morning.

Oddly, you could see quite well that he was genuinely
   glad –
As if, in fact, he had been actually looking forward to this
   Sunday service,
Much the way I had been looking forward to it myself;
As if, in fact, this was the big moment of his day – of his
   week,
Not merely another ritual to be sanctimoniously performed.
He was a small, stocky, handsome man in his forties
With a big mop of curly grey hair
And black, horn-rimmed, tinted spectacles.
I am sure that more than half the women in the church
Fell in love with him on the spot –
Not to mention the men.
Myself, I felt like a cuddle.
The reading from the prophet Ezekiel (17: 22–24)
Was a lot of old codswallop about cedar trees in Israel
(It's a long way from a tin of steak-and-kidney pie
For Sunday lunch in a Dublin bedsit
To cedar trees in Israel),
And the epistle was even worse –

St Paul on his high horse and, as nearly always,
Putting his hoof in it – prating about 'the law court of Christ'
(Director of Public Prosecutions, Mr J. Christ, Messiah)!
With the Gospel, however, things began to look up –
The parable of the mustard seed as being the kingdom of
    heaven;
Now then the Homily, at best probably inoffensively
    boring.

It's Father's Day – this small, solid, serious, sexy priest
    began –
And I want to tell you about my own father
Because none of you knew him.
If there was one thing he liked, it was a pint of Guinness;
If there was one thing he liked more than a pint of Guinness
It was two pints of Guinness.
But then when he was fifty-five he gave up drink.
I never knew why, but I had my suspicions.
Long after he had died my mother told me why:
He was so proud of me when I entered the seminary
That he gave up drinking as his way of thanking God.
But he himself never said a word about it to me –
He kept his secret to the end. He died from cancer
A few weeks before I was ordained a priest.
I'd like to go to Confession – he said to me:
OK – I'll go and get a priest – I said to him:
No – don't do that – I'd prefer to talk to *you:*
Dying, he confessed to me the story of his life.
How many of you here at Mass today are fathers?
I want all of you who are fathers to stand up.

Not one male in transept or aisle or nave stood up –
It was as if all the fathers in the church had been caught out
In the profanity of their sanctity,
In the bodily nakedness of their fatherhood,
In the carnal deed of their fathering;
Then, in ones and twos and threes, fifty or sixty of us

    clambered to our feet
And blushed to the roots of our being.
Now – declared the priest – let the rest of us
Praise these men our fathers.
He began to clap hands.
Gradually the congregation began to clap hands,
Until the entire church was ablaze with clapping hands –
Wives vying with daughters, sons with sons,
Clapping clapping clapping clapping clapping,
While I stood there in a trance, tears streaming down my
    cheeks:
Jesus!
I want to tell you about my own father
Because none of you knew him!

PART
II

Hymn to a Broken Marriage

Dear Nessa – Now that our marriage is over
I would like you to know that, if I could put back the clock
Fifteen years to the cold March day of our wedding,
I would wed you again and, if that marriage also broke,
I would wed you yet again and, if it a third time broke,
Wed you again, and again, and again, and again, and again:
If you would have me which, of course, you would not
For, even you – in spite of your patience and your innocence
(Strange characteristics in an age such as our own) –
Even you require to shake off the addiction of romantic love
And seek, instead, the herbal remedy of a sane affection
In which are mixed in profuse and fair proportion
Loverliness, brotherliness, fatherliness:
A sane man could not espouse a more intimate friend than
    you.

The Jewish Bride

(after Rembrandt)

At the black canvas of estrangement,
As the smoke empties from the ruins under a gold
    Winter sky,
Death-trains clattering across the back gardens of
    Amsterdam
– Sheds, buckets, wire, concrete
– Manholes, pumps, pliers, scaffolding;
I see, as if for the first time,
The person you were, and are, and always will be
Despite the evil that men do:
The teenage girl on the brink of womanhood
Who, when I met you, was on the brink of everything –
Composing fairytales and making drawings
That used remind your friends of Anderson and Thurber –
Living your hidden life that promised everything
Despite all the maimed, unreliable men and women
Who were at that moment congregating all around you:
Including, of course, most of all, myself.
You made of your bedroom a flowing stream
Into which, daily, you threw proofs of your dreams;
Pinned to your bedroom wall with brass-studded
    drawing pins
Newspaper and magazine photographs of your heroes and
    heroines.
People who met you breathed the air of freedom,
And sensuality fragile as it was wild:
'Nessa's air makes free' people used say,
Like in the dark ages, 'Town air makes free'.
The miracle is that you survived me.
You stroll about the malls and alleyways of Amsterdam,
About its islands and bridges, its archways and jetties,
With Spring in your heels, although it is Winter;
Privately, publicly, along the Grand Parade;

A Jewish Bride who has survived the death-camp,
Free at last of my swastika eyes
Staring at you from across spiked dinner plates
Or from out of the bunker of a TV armchair;
Free of the glare off my jackboot silence;
Free of the hysteria of my gestapo voice;
Now your shyness replenished with all your old cheeky
    confidence –
That grassy well at which red horses used rear up and sip
With young men naked riding bareback calling your name.
Dog-muzzle of tension torn down from your face;
Black polythene of asphyxiation peeled away from your
    soul;
Your green eyes quivering with dark, sunny laughter
And – all spread-eagled and supple again – your loving,
    freckled hands.

Around the Corner from Francis Bacon

Around the corner from Francis Bacon
Was where we made our first nest together
On the waters of the flood;
Where we first lived in sin:
The sunniest, most virtuous days of our life.
Not even the pastoral squalor of Clapham Common
Nor the ghetto life of Notting Hill Gate
Nor the racial drama of Barcelona
Nor the cliffhanging bourgeois life of Cork City
Could ever equal those initial, primeval times together
Living in sin
In the halcyon ambience of South Kensington,
A haven for peaceful revolutionaries such as Harriet Waugh
Or Francis Bacon, or ourselves.
I slept on an ironing board in the kitchen
And you slept in the attic:
Late at night when all the other flat-dwellers
Were abed and – we thought wishfully – asleep,
You crept down the attic ladder
To make love with me on the ironing board,
As if we had known each other in a previous life
So waterily did our two body-phones attune,
Underwater swimming face to face in the dark,
Francis Bacon-Cimabue style.
My body-phone was made in Dublin
But your body-phone was made in Japan.
Standing up naked on the kitchen floor,
In the smog-filtered moonlight,
You placed your hand on my little folly, murmuring:
I have come to iron you, Sir Board.
Far from the tyrant liberties of Dublin, Ireland,
Where the comedy of freedom was by law forbidden
And truth, since the freedom of the state, gone
    underground.
When you had finished ironing me

I felt like hot silk queueing up to be bathèd
Under a waterfall in Samarkand
Or a mountain stream in Enniskerry.
Every evening I waited for you to come home,
Nipping out only in the rush hour to the delicatessen
Where Francis Bacon, basket under arm,
Surfacing like Mr Mole from his mews around the corner,
Used be stocking up in tomato purée and curry powder
Before heading off into the night and 'The Colony Room
    Club'
Into whose green dark you and I sometimes also tip-toed.
In your own way you were equally Beatrix Potter-like,
Coming home to me laden with fish fingers and baked
    beans.
While I read to you from Dahlberg, you taught me about the
    psyche
Of the female orang-outang caged in the zoo:
Coronation Street. . . Z Cars. . . The World in Action . . .
Then Z Cars to beat all Z Cars – our own world in action –
The baskets of your eyes chock-a-block with your unique
    brands
Of tomato purée and curry powder;
Or, *That Was The Week That Was*, and then, my sleeping
    friend,
In the sandhills of whose shoulders sloping secretly down
Into small, hot havens of pure unscathèd sands
Where the only sounds are the sounds of the sea's tidal
    waters
Flooding backwards and forwards,
Tonight is the night that always is forever –
Ten or twenty minutes in the dark,
And in four million years or so
My stomach will swarm again suddenly with butterflies,
As with your bowl of water and your towel,
Your candle and your attic ladder,
Your taut high wire and your balancing pole,
A green mini-dress over your arm, a Penguin paperback in
    your hand,

I watch you coming towards me in the twilight of rush hour
On your hands and knees
And on the wet, mauve tip of your extended tongue
The two multi-coloured birds of your plumed eyes ablaze
Around the corner from Francis Bacon.

'Windfall', 8 Parnell Hill, Cork

But, then, at the end of the day I could always say –
Well, now, I am going home:
I felt elected, steeped, sovereign to be able to say –
I am going home.
When I was at home I liked to stay at home;
At home I stayed at home for weeks;
At home I used sit in a winged chair by the window
Overlooking the river and the factory chimneys,
The electricity power station and the car assembly works,
The fleets of trawlers and the pilot tugs,
Dreaming that life is a dream which is real,
The river a reflection of itself in its own waters,
Goya sketching Goya among the smoky mirrors.
The industrial vista was my Mont Sainte-Victoire;
While my children sat on my knees watching TV
Their mother, my wife, reclined on the couch
Knitting a bright-coloured scarf, drinking a cup of black
    coffee,
Smoking a cigarette – one of her own roll-ups.
I closed my eyes and breathed in and breathed out.
It is ecstasy to breathe if you are at home in the world.
What a windfall! A home of our own!
Our neighbours' houses had names like 'Con Amore',
'Sans Souci', 'Pacelli', 'Montini', 'Homesville';
But we called our home 'Windfall':
'Windfall', 8 Parnell Hill, Cork.
In the gut of my head coursed the leaf of tranquillity
Which I dreamed was known only to Buddhist Monks
In lotus monasteries high up in the Hindu Kush.
Down here in the dark depths of Ireland,
Below sea-level in the city of Cork,
In a city as intimate and homicidal as a Little Marseilles,
In a country where all the children of the nation
Are not cherished equally
And where the best go homeless, while the worst

Erect block-house palaces – self-regardingly ugly,
Having a home of your own can give to a family
A chance in a lifetime to transcend death.

At the high window, shipping from all over the world
Being borne up and down the busy, yet contemplative,
    river;
Skylines drifting in and out of skylines in the cloudy valley;
Firelight at dusk, and city lights in the high window,
Beyond them the control tower of the airport on the hill
– A lighthouse in the sky flashing green to white to green;
Our black-and-white cat snoozing in the corner of a chair;
Pastels and etchings on the four walls, and over the
    mantelpiece
Van Gogh's Grave and *Lovers in Water*;
A room wallpapered in books and family photograph
    albums
Chronicling the adventures and metamorphoses of family
    life:
In swaddling clothes in Mammy's arms on baptism day;
Being a baby of nine months and not remembering it;
Face-down in a pram, incarcerated in a high chair;
Everybody, including strangers, wearing shop-window
    smiles;
With Granny in Felixstowe, with Granny in Ballymaloo;
In a group photo in First Infants, on a bike at thirteen;
In the back garden in London, in the back garden in Cork;
Performing a headstand after First Holy Communion;
Getting a kiss from the Bishop on Confirmation Day;
Straw hats in the Bois de Boulogne, wearing wings at the
    seaside;
Mammy and Daddy holding hands on the Normandy
    Beaches;
Mammy and Daddy at the wedding of Jeremiah and
    Margot;
Mammy and Daddy queueing up for *Last Tango in Paris*;
Boating on the Shannon, climbing mountains in Kerry;
Building sandcastles in Killala, camping in Barley Cove;

Picnicking in Moone, hide-and-go-seek in Clonmacnoise;
Riding horses, cantering, jumping fences;
Pushing out toy yachts in the pond in the Tuileries;
The Irish College revisited in the Rue des Irlandais;
Sipping an *orange pressé* through a straw on the roof of the
    Beaubourg;
Dancing in Père Lachaise, weeping at Auvers.
Year in, year out, I pored over these albums accumulating,
My children looking over my shoulder, exhilarated as I was,
Their mother presiding at our ritual from a distance
– The far side of the hearthrug, diffidently, proudly:
Schoolbooks on the floor and pyjamas on the couch –
Whose turn is it tonight to put the children to bed?

Our children swam about our home
As if it was their private sea,
Their own unique, symbiotic fluid
Of which their parents also partook.
Such is home – a sea of your own –
In which you hang upside down from the ceiling
With equanimity, while postcards from Thailand on the
    mantelpiece
Are raising their eyebrow markings benignly:
Your hands dangling their prayers to the floorboards of
    your home,
Sifting the sands underneath the surfaces of conversations,
The marine insect life of the family psyche.
A home of your own – or a sea of your own –
In which climbing the walls is as natural
As making love on the stairs;
In which when the telephone rings
Husband and wife are metamorphosed into smiling
    accomplices,
Both declining to answer it;
Initiating, instead, a yet more subversive kiss
– A kiss they have perhaps never attempted before –
And might never have dreamed of attempting

Were it not for the telephone belling.
Through the bannisters or along the bannister rails
The pyjama-clad children solemnly watching
Their parents at play, jump up and down in support,
Race back to bed, gesticulating wordlessly:
The most subversive unit in society is the human family.

We're almost home, pet, almost home. . .
Our home is at. . .
I'll be home. . .
I have to go home now. . .
I want to go home now. . .
Are you feeling homesick?. . .
Are you anxious to get home?. . .
I can't wait to get home. . .
Let's stay at home tonight and. . .
What time will you be coming home at?. . .
If I'm not home by six at the latest, I'll phone. . .
We're nearly home, don't worry, we're nearly home. . .

But then with good reason
I was put out of my home:
By a keen wind felled.
I find myself now without a home
Having to live homeless in the alien, foreign city of Dublin.
It is an eerie enough feeling to be homesick
Yet knowing you will be going home next week;
It is an eerie feeling beyond all ornithological analysis
To be homesick knowing that there is no home to go
    home to:
Day by day, creeping, crawling,
Moonlighting, escaping,
Bed-and-breakfast to bed-and-breakfast;
Hostels, centres, one-night hotels.

Homeless in Dublin,
Blown about the suburban streets at evening,

Peering in the windows of other people's homes,
Wondering what it must feel like
To be sitting around a fire –
Apache or Cherokee or Bourgeoisie –
Beholding the firelit faces of your family,
Beholding their starry or their TV gaze:
Windfall to Windfall – can you hear me?
Windfall to Windfall. . .
We're almost home pet, don't worry anymore, we're almost
    home.

Cleaning Ashtrays

We were as hung-up on one another as Romeo and Juliet,
Not only in the days of our courtship
But after fifteen years of matrimony
(Only the week before she left me
She held me in her arms on the boat deck
Of the Cork-Swansea Ferry,
Pledging eternal love to one another,
The lifeboats above our heads as solid as ever,
Permanent fixtures – only wholly symbolic);
Yet our love-cries in the night had grown infrequent
And she had multiplied the numbers of cigarettes she
    smoked.
After she went out to work, and the children to school,
I stood in the kitchen cleaning ashtrays;
The spectacle of a kitchen sink with encrusted ashtrays
Piled-up with tap water dripping into the scum
Made me fear her with a fierce, irrational fear.
As I scoured the ashtrays with my bare fingers
I swore I'd smash these evil receptacles on the kitchen floor
If she'd not mend her ways and give up the fags.
I interpreted each rim of wet black ash
As a personal insult to my individual being
Which she – concerned to ontologically annihilate me –
Had deliberately contrived by continuing to smoke
While reading, to cause me more pain, Jean Paul Sartre.
What chance had nervous chain-smoking Juliet
When Romeo cleaning ashtrays had such thoughts?
If only Romeo had been more ethical, less romantic,
He might have thought more of love, less of self,
And planted in her lips such petalled fires
As she would have had no need to inhale tobacco.
Now Julietless, how Romeo pines for all those days and
    nights
Cleaning ashtrays – cleaning ashtrays for his only Juliet.

Raymond of the Rooftops

The morning after the night
The roof flew off the house
And our sleeping children narrowly missed
Being decapitated by falling slates,
I asked my husband if he would
Help me put back the roof:
But no – he was too busy at his work
Writing for a women's magazine in London
An Irish Fairytale called *Raymond of the Rooftops*.
Will you have a heart, woman – he bellowed –
Can't you see I am up to my eyes and ears in work,
Breaking my neck to finish *Raymond of the Rooftops*,
Fighting against time to finish *Raymond of the Rooftops*,
Putting everything I have got into *Raymond of the Rooftops*?

Isn't it well for him? *Everything he has got!*

All I wanted him to do was to stand
For an hour, maybe two hours, three at the most,
At the bottom of the stepladder
And hand me up slates while I slated the roof:
But no – once again I was proving to be the insensitive,
Thoughtless, feckless even, wife of the artist.
There was I up to my fat, raw knees in rainwater
Worrying him about the hole in our roof
While he was up to his neck in *Raymond of the Rooftops*.
Will you have a heart, woman – he bellowed –
Can't you see I am up to my eyes and ears in work,
Breaking my neck to finish *Raymond of the Rooftops*,
Fighting against time to finish *Raymond of the Rooftops*,
Putting everything I have got into *Raymond of the Rooftops*?

Isn't it well for him? *Everything he has got!*

The Day my Wife Purchased Herself a Handgun

It was not so much that I minded her purchasing a handgun
(Although of course I did mind – deep down I knew
That it was against nature for a woman to purchase a
    handgun –
Above all, it was against nature for a wife-woman to
    purchase a handgun):
What I vehemently objected to was her laid-back habit at
    bedtime
Of leaving her handgun strewn about on top of her
    underwear.
I felt strongly that if she had to have a gun at all
She ought obey the proprieties and keep it concealed in a
    drawer:
There are many indignities which a husband ought to be
    spared.
But she had always kept an untidy, lived-in type bedroom –
The class of woman who appears to get a kick
Out of showering her underwear in a heap on the floor –
But, as if all that were not penitential enough
For a husband to have to put up with,
What I now had to endure night after night
Was the same old variety show of her braided black bra,
Her black silk slip, her black nylon tights,
And her frilly green panties, all topped off by a handgun.

Frantic, I leapt out of bed and confronted myself:
But when I looked in the mirror I was not there.
Thereafter, whenever she attempted to speak to me,
I always used say 'Sorry I am not here'
And put the phone down, unable to say that I was.
Finally, then, when she got herself a pair of hand grenades
And took to scattering them desultorily around the sacred
    bedroom
With the pins out,

I went off the deep end altogether
And cut the telephone wires attaching *my* eyes to *her* eyes.
If it's one thing a wife must not do, it's to grow up:
A man will endure anything – except a grown-up woman.

The Pietà's Over

The Pietà's Over – and, now, my dear, droll, husband,
As middle age tolls its bell along the via dolorosa of life,
It is time for you to get down off my knees
And learn to walk on your own two feet.
I will admit it is difficult for a man of forty
Who has spent all his life reclining in his wife's lap,
Being given birth to by her again and again, year in, year
     out,
To stand on his own two feet, but it has to be done –
Even if at the end of the day he commits harikari.
A man cannot be a messiah for ever,
Messiahing about in his wife's lap,
Suffering fluently in her arms,
Flowing up and down in the lee of her bosom,
Forever being mourned for by the eternal feminine,
Being keened over every night of the week for sixty mortal
     years.

The Pietà's Over – it is Easter over all our lives:
The revelation of our broken marriage, and its resurrection;
The breaking open of the tomb, and the setting free.
Painful as it was for me, I put you down off my knee
And I showed you the door.
Although you pleaded with me to keep you on my knee
And to mollycoddle you, humour you, within the family
     circle
('Don't put me out into the cold world' you cried),
I did not take the easy way out and yield to you –
Instead I took down the door off its hinges
So that the sunlight shone all the more squarely
Upon the pure, original brokenness of our marriage;
I whispered to you, quietly, yet audibly,
For all the diaspora of your soul to hear:
The Pietà's Over.

54

Yet even now, one year later, you keep looking back
From one side of Europe to the other,
Gaping at my knees as if my knees
Were the source of all that you have been, are, or will be.
By all means look around you, but stop looking back.
I would not give you shelter if you were homeless in the
    streets
For you must make your home in yourself, and not in a
    woman.
Keep going out the road for it is only out there –
Out there where the river achieves its riverlessness –
That you and I can become at last strangers to one another,
Ready to join up again on Resurrection Day.
Therefore, I must keep whispering to you, over and over:
My dear loved one, I have to tell you,
You have run the gamut of piety –
The Pietà's Over.

Wives May Be Coveted But Not by Their Husbands

We lived in a remote dower house in Cork
Leaving the doors and windows always unlocked.
When herds of deer came streaming through the kitchen
At first we laughed, but then we quarrelled –
As the years went by, we quarrelled more than laughed:
'You seem to care more about deer than about me' –
'I am weary of subsisting in an eyrie of antlers' –
'Be a man and erect a fence' –
'Be a woman and put venison in the pot'.
When an old gold stag dawdled by her rocking chair
And she caressed his warm hide with smiling hands,
I locked myself in the attic and sulked for weeks.
Stags, does, and fauns, grew thick around her bed
As in her bloom of life she evolved, alone.

Death-Camp

(after Frankl)

It is crucial that never a day should pass
That I do not recollect my comportment in death-camp:
Staring out through the barbed wire
I see on the tangled point of a barb
The smiling face of my wife in the burnt, sulphurous air;
In the slime of my shame I see her smiling face –
She who was turned into lampshades six months ago
On my say-so, when as Camp Commandant of Treblinka
I locked myself into a tiny white world of pure evil
Until I myself was arrested and deported to Birkenau.
Nothing now that the Camp Commandant can do
Can stop me from seeing my wife smiling on the barbed wire.
Day in, day out, such knowledge is the most precious secret
    of all:
I carry it with me all the days of my burning.

The Turkish Carpet

No man could have been more unfaithful
To his wife than me;
Scarcely a day passed
That I was not unfaithful to her.
I would be in the living-room ostensibly reading or writing
When she'd come home from work unexpectedly early
And, popping her head round the door, find me
    wrapped round
A figure of despair.
It would not have been too bad if I'd been wrapped round
Another woman – that would have been infidelity of a kind
With which my wife could have coped.
What she could not cope with, try as she did,
Was the infidelity of unhope,
The personal betrayal of universal despair.
When my wife called to me from the living-room door
Tremblingly ajar, with her head peering round it,
– The paintwork studded with headwounds and
    knuckleprints –
Called to me across the red, red grass of home
– *The Turkish Carpet* –
Which her gay mother had given us as a wedding present
(And on which our children had so often played
Dolls' Houses on their hands and knees
And headstands and cartwheels and dances,
And on which we ourselves had so often made love),
I clutched my despair to my breast
And with brutality kissed it – Sweet Despair –
Staring red-eyed down at *The Turkish Carpet*.
O my dear husband, will you not be faithful to me?
Have I not given you hope all the days of my life?

Girls Playing with Boys

My wife-to-be used play in the front garden
In the grass and the gravel with the boys next-door.
A small red-headed girl,
She loved playing with boys;
She loved playing, and she loved boys,
And when she put the two together
She got 'playing with boys',
And naturally she thought
That boys would be boys
And playing would be playing,
And since girls were girls
'Girls Playing with Boys'
Would be the most natural game of all –
The number one game in the world.

Girls Playing with Boys

How was my wife-to-be to know
That she was also to be my ex-wife to-be?
Yet, as she played on her own in the front garden
And dreamed about the little boys next-door –
Whatever did they do with those pretty little
Yokemebobs between their boney legs? –
She sensed among the scatter of broken daisy chains
Something else besides the smell of summer grass.

Girls Playing with Boys

So it was she had the courage to make breaks,
And made of our marriage a truly broken marriage.
Only then did she achieve her potential as a human being,
Her incomplete completion as a small red-headed girl –
Only then did I see her for the spirit that she is.
I could not believe it as she walked away from me
As I sat watching on TV a funeral in Moscow,

Slumped in my armchair in disbelief.
I felt sure she would cling to the Church-State lie
Of the happy, wholesome, white teeth marriage:
I did not believe she would have the nerve to *break* –
Although I had always known her to be a courageous
    woman,
More courageous by far
Than those whom the world deems brave:
She makes jellyfish guerrillas look frail
And bullylike – in their revulsion to change.

I loved my wife – although I say it myself –
And yet it was not until the day she left me
– *Girls Playing with Boys* –
That I began to see that she was not
First of all a woman and, second of all, a human being:
Her soul stepped out of its furry pelt
(Woman-image patented by archbishops and film directors)
And I saw her, as if for the first time, in the glittering dusk,
Standing alone on the dual carriageway outside Cork City –
Her two children waiting for her in her car –
Lighting up a cigarette, chatting to a motorcycle cop;
A solitary, vulnerable, detached, beautiful human being
Sharing a risky joke with a motorcycle cop;
A girl playing with a boy – playing for playing:
For her there is only the playing – all else is death.

The Berlin Wall Café

Once we were Berlin – you and I. . .
Until an agèd priest,
As shepherdlike a pastor as one could hope to meet
In the neon forest –
Father Boniface –
Married us with a gun.
Tears of joy were in his eyes as, with a flick of his wrist
(All mottled and bluey),
He waved his pistol in the air, firing gaily:
A long white wall unfurled from it,
Trailing its roll-top and its graffiti.

Thus it was we pitched our tent in the continuing city:
Ecstatically lonely together in a two-room flat
In Bernauer Strasse beside the Berlin Wall,
Around the corner from the open-air table tennis tables
In Swinemünder Strasse,
Handy for the *U-Bahn* in Volta Strasse.
I counted myself the luckiest man alive in Berlin
To be marooned with you:
You – incarnate coincidence of the beautiful and the true –
All risk and give –
Reticent woman whose eyes were caves
Concealed in cascades of red hair.
Yet all I could talk about was the Berlin Wall
As if the Berlin Wall was more important than you!
On the night you gave birth to our child
I was too busy to attend – addressing a meeting
On the Berlin Wall!
When I should have been cooking your supper
After your long day's work in the office in Spandau,
I was manning the Observation Platforms –
Making faces at the *Volkspolizei!*

At the end of 1980,
When I should have been minding our marriage
And concentrating on loving you,
All I could consider was whether or not
I should become Editor of the *Berlin Wall Gazette*:
I was a most proper Charlie!
No wonder that your friends could not abide me!
Whenever they saw me approaching they scattered:
'Watch out – here he comes – Checkpoint Charlie'.

In 1984 you could stand it no more:
You escaped from West Berlin
Into East Berlin – where you are free of me
And of the Show Biz of the Free Democracies
Advertising Unemployment and All That Jazz.
Purple with envy, I hear you have teamed up
With an all-woman jazz combo in Unter den Linden.
They say there's no more exciting woman in Berlin
Than when you're alone on the high-hat cymbals
To beat the band in the Berlin Wall Café:
Once we were Berlin – you and I. . .

The Marriage Contract

She is the kind of person
(The kind of person I like)
Who never reads the small print in contracts:
E.g. – where it says 'he's a xenophobic psychopath',
She took no notice, taking me at face value.

Today – our broken marriage broken –
Busybodies are quick to tell her
What a noble, handsome soul she is
And what a bowsy her ex-husband was:
But she has no time for these
Soothsayers of the marriage contract,
She being an anarchist herself –
With always, at the worst of times,
Dreams of good times;
And with always, at the best of times,
Memories of bad times.
Besides, it is of no piquancy to her now
To be told that her husband
Was a retarded third-degree necrophiliac:
She remembers him as he was,
Warts and all,
The man she loved and the man she married.
The warts bloomed in swarms
Quite naturally over the years
Until there were simply too many of them.
She took a second glance at the contract,
And realised that it had run out.
Afterwards, she gave it to him as a souvenir
Knowing his passion for such memorabilia:
By the light of a TV programme he was not watching
– A black-and-white film of *King Lear* with the sound turned
    down –
He sunk it into the frontal lobes of his brain,
Like a blank cheque from God sunk into stone.

The Vasectomy Bureau at Lisdoonvarna

Concerning the predicament of naked priests in cold pulpits
Preaching to fully-clothed couples in double beds
How birth should be controlled or, rather, not controlled –
I would like to pour more oil on troubled waters
And to whisper – through lips that have never kissed a
    bishop's lips –
That I am ill-at-ease with men
Who think they know best what women ought do:
Men who intone poppycock to their wives about rhythm,
Or men such as myself who prescribed the pill
Until my wife's heart almost stopped beating.

Instead what I should like to see
Down by the hazel wood, or the dark lake fair,
Is a bureau for vasectomy:
Down at Lisdoonvarna, not far from the sea,
Where men are women, and women are men.

Man, you have popped your poppycock for long enough –
My wife declared to me as she emptied a packet of
    contraceptive pills
Down the lavatory bowl.
(Thereby derailing my sense of decorum –
Oh my precious male sense of decorum!
What you may, or may not, pour down a lavatory bowl:
Bowel deposits, yes – contraceptive pills, no.
Who knows what strange babies might get conceived in
    sewers
And foul up the entire sewerage of our moral system?)

Tearing up our marriage contract with a wistful smile
And tying a loose noose of rhythm around my neck
As I dangled by my ankles from my social values,
My wife walked sideways out the front door,
In clogs,

64

On a pair of stilts,
In topless trousers
Beneath her busman's cap,
To begin a new life by the Western Sea,
With a Norwegian who has the courage of his King Canutes
As well as of his convictions.
Yet even now there are, between the crevices in the
    limestone desert
Down at Lisdoonvarna,
Little Victories, Bloody Cranesbills, Vasectomies:
Tiny Alpine wildflowers, survivors of ice ages.

At the Funeral of the Marriage

At the funeral of the marriage
My wife and I paced
On either side of the hearse,
Our children racing behind it. . .
As the coffin was emptied
Down into the bottomless grave,
Our children stood in a half-circle,
Playing on flutes and recorders.
My wife and I held hands.
While the mourners wept and the gravediggers
Unfurled shovelfuls of clay
Down on top of the coffin,
We slowly walked away,
Accomplices beneath the yew trees.
We had a cup of tea in the graveyard café
Across the street from the gates:
We discussed the texture of the undertaker's face,
Its beetroot quality.
As I gazed at my wife
I wondered who on earth she was –
I saw that she was a green-eyed stranger.
I said to her: Would you like to go to a film?
She said: I would love to go to a film.
In the back seats of the cinema,
As we slid up and down in our seats
In a frenzy of hooks and clasps,
The manager courteously asked us not to take off our clothes.
We walked off urgently through the rain-strewn streets
Into a leaf-sodden cul-de-sac
And as, from the tropic isle of our bed,
Chock-a-block with sighs & cries,
We threw our funeral garments on the floor,
We could hear laughter outside the door.
There is no noise children love more to hear
Than the noise of their parents making love:
O my darling, who on earth are you?

On Falling in Love with a Salesman in a Shoeshop

I live in a room with no windows:
Weeks go by with but a memory of daylight
Trickling under the door.
After one such week under a naked light bulb,
Crouched by a gas fire in a torn-up armchair
Whose springs have all gasped their last gasp,
I emerged into daylight in order to purchase
A new pair of shoes.
There was no need for me to purchase a new pair of shoes,
But I felt that if I did purchase a new pair of shoes
I would somehow feel better
About the world, for in my experience
The world is not the sort of place
I would choose to inhabit
If I had had any choice in the matter.
I am so cold I have to sleep in my overcoat,
And there is three inches of water on the kitchen floor.
There was a young man in the shop,
Not my type at all,
A brisk, athletic, TV advertisement sort of chap:
But his matter-of-fact gentleness,
His courtesy,
Shocked me.
After I had picked out a pair of watertight shoes,
He invited me to sit down beside him on a bench
And to talk with him about the new situation:
There we sat alone in the shoeshop
While the world marched up and down outside
Like the Grand Old Duke of York
(For whom, I may say, I have an old affection
From the days when I used discuss him with my baby
    daughters);
There we sat alone in the shoeshop
Discussing shoes – discussing watertight shoes.
When I came out of the shop

I could not stand still;
When I got back to my bedsit
I put my feet in a basin of hot water,
A red plastic basin of hot water,
And I closed my eyes and dreamed
Of what it would be like
To love and be loved –
To die of it.
I wish that my wife,
Instead of leaving me,
Had taken my head in her hands
And put it into a basin of water
And kept it deep down there until dead.
On the other hand, if the shoe salesman were to marry me,
I suppose that he would also probably leave me.

The Vision of St Hubert

(after Breughel)

I decided to hunt down my wife:
Gauleiters of Revenge revved-up in my veins
Egged on by Storm-Troopers of Greed;
I gathered round me all my Dogs of Self-Pity,
Long, lean, Bloodhounds of Self-Pity,
Black-and-white fellows with pointed wet snouts,
And into the city we plunged –
Where I knew she had been hidden away
By her friends in a Jewish ghetto.
Tonight I would hunt down my wife –
She who had taken from me
My home and my children,
She who had taken from me herself!
What right had she who belonged to me
To take from me herself?
If, with tears and fears, she has the neck
To exhibit herself as the hapless doe with her fauns,
I will prove myself to be more than a stag for her:
I will put the fear of God the Führer into her
And smear the walls of her bedroom with the blood of her
    children;
I will prove myself to be a true male savage, three-leggèd
    and merciless.

It was not difficult to hunt her down:
I rode around the rooftops of the city
Until I unearthed her, with her children,
In a bedroom on a cliff overlooking the city.
Go away from me, Hubert! – she cried
And, as she cried it out again and again,
Go away from me, Hubert, go away from me!
I heard in her cry her voice:
Her voice that last I'd heard when first we'd met –

Seventeen odd years ago.
In the seventeen odd years
Since we'd first met and married
I had never listened to her voice,
Listening out only for the voice of my wife.

World, I'd like to introduce you to my wife –
Oh Hubert, don't talk like a jumped-up pimp.

But now as I heard her voice in her voice
I fell in love with her, as it was in the beginning:
I got down off my high horse and knelt at her feet
In the bedroom doorway, and while all my murderous
Drunken accomplices of the night melted away,
Dawn lit up the chimney-stack skyline of Cork City;
And while our two sleeping children clasped in their hands
Close up to their foreheads a frog and a lizard,
Calmly I pledged her my prayer and affection,
Promising her never again to seek her out,
Never again in this city to darken her doorway,
To woo her only and always in the eternity of my loss:
Let us now praise famous women – and their children.